1000 SIGHT WORDS
THE ULTIMATE
VOCABULARY BOOK

PICTURE DICTIONARY WITH SENTENCE

English - Czech

action

akce

Action!

actually

vlastně

I actually like strawberry.

adjective

jméno

Tell me an adjective to describe this.

afraid

strach

What are you afraid of?

agreed

souhlasil

They agreed on music.

ahead

vpřed

Who was ahead in the race?

allow

dovolit

Did the teacher allow him to go play?

apple

jablko

Eat an apple.

arrived

dorazil

My plane arrived on time.

born

narozený

Where were you born?

bought

koupil

She bought new clothes.

British

britský

Who is the British monarch?

capital

hlavní město

The capital is in Washington DC.

chance

šance

Dice is a game of chance.

chart

zmapovat

What does your medical chart say?

church

kostel

Did you go to church?

column

sloupec

Did you read the newspaper column?

company

společnost

What company do you work for?

conditions

podmínky

What are the weather conditions.

corn

kukuřice

Do you like corn?

cotton

bavlna

A q-tip is made of cotton.

cows

kráva

How many cows does he have?

create

vytvořit

What art did you create?

dead

mrtvý

The bug is dead.

deal

obchod

Did you agree on the deal?

death

smrt

The grim reaper is death.

details

podrobnosti

Look for the details.

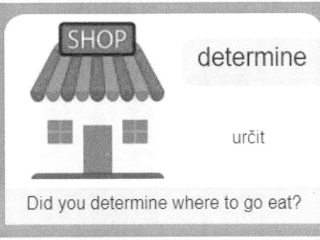

determine

určit

Did you determine where to go eat?

difficult

obtížný

I found this difficult.

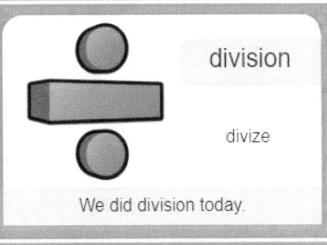

division

divize

We did division today.

doesn't

ne

Doesn't it sound beautiful?

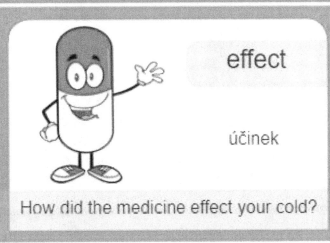

effect

účinek

How did the medicine effect your cold?

entire

celý

The entire family was in the picture.

especially

zvláštní

She especially liked writing.

evening

večer

The ceremony was this evening.

experience

zkušenosti

She has a lot of experience.

factories

továrny

There are a lot of factories there.

fair

zábavní park

Let's go to the fair.

fear

strach

I have a huge fear of clowns.

fig

fíky

I ate a fig.

forward

vpřed

Spring forward the clocks.

France

francie

Have you ever been to France?

fresh

čerstvý

All the fruit is fresh.

Greek

řecký

Have you ever had Greek food?

gun

zbraně

We played with a water gun.

hoe

motyka

Use a hoe in the garden.

huge

obrovský

Those trees are huge!

isn't

není

Isn't it nice to hang out with friends?

led

vůdce

The dog led her.

level

úroveň

Use the level to hang the picture.

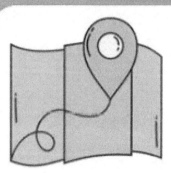

located

nachází se

Where is the store located?

march

průvod

Are you going to march with the band?

match

vhodný

Did you match them?

molecules

molekuly

Are those molecules?

northern

severní

He lives in northern California.

nose

nos

My nose is running.

office

kancelář

Do you need any office supplies?

oxygen

kyslík

What is the symbol for oxygen?

plural

množný

What is the plural of a mouse?

prepared

připravit

She prepared for the exam.

pretty

dosti

Pretty in pink.

printed

tištěné

She printed out the forms.

radio

rádio

Let's listen to the radio.

repeated

opakovat

They repeated the exercises daily.

rope

lano

Do you have any rope?

rose

růže

Thank you for the rose.

score

skóre

What was the final score?

seat

sedadlo

The girls took a seat in the sand.

settled

se usadil

The case was settled.

shoes

obuv

Put your shoes on.

shop

obchody

I'm need to go shop for groceries.

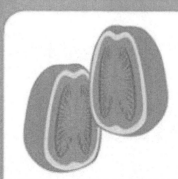

similar

podobný

The halves are similar.

sir

vážený pane

Yes, sir!

sister

sestra

Is she your sister?

smell

vůně

I love the smell of cookies!

solution

řešení

I figured out a solution!

southern

jižní

She's a southern belle.

steel

ocel

The new building used steel.

stretched

natažené

We stretched before the workout.

substances

látky

What are these substances?

suffix

přípona

What is the suffix of the word?

sugar

cukr

Sugar cube for your tea?

tools

nástroje

May I borrow your tools?

total

colkový

What's the total?

track

dráha

The runners got on the track.

triangle

trojúhelník

How many sides does a triangle have?

truck

náklaďák

Is thaty our truck?

underline
<u>underline</u>
zdůraznit

Underline the word.

various

rozličný

I watch various shows.

view

pohled

That is a beautiful view!

Washington

washington

She is from Washington.

we'll

vůle

We'll finish buying our groceries.

western

západní

It's western wear day.

win

vyhrát

Did you win?

woman

žena

The woman was on her way to work.

workers

pracovník

The workers were busy.

wouldn't

ne

Wouldn't you like to go shopping?

wrong

špatně

Did I get it wrong?

yellow

žlutá

A banana is yellow.

after

po

You may have dessert after dinner.

again

znovu

May we go on the ride again?

air

vzduch

The air was cold.

also

taky

I also like baseball.

America

amerika

Columbus sailed to America.

animal

zvíře

My favorite animal is a lion.

another

další

Have another cookie.

answer

odpovědět

Raise your hand to answer.

any

žádný

Do you have any crayons?

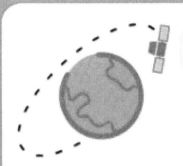

around

kolem

Let's travel around the world.

ask

dotázat se

It's good to ask questions.

away

pryč

Throw your trash away.

back

zadní

We went back to school.

because

protože

I went to bed because I was tired.

before

před

Sharpen your pencil before the test.

big

velký

The elephant is a big animal.

boy

chlapec

The boy played a basketball.

came

přišel

He came to class.

change

změna

I save my change.

different

odlišný

They use different balls.

does

dělat

Does he ride the bus?

end

konec

She watched to the end.

even

dokonce

They learned about even numbers.

follow

následovat

Follow the teacher.

form

formulář

Complete the form.

found

nalezeno

We found a puppy.

give

dát

I like to give gifts.

good

dobrý

The hamburger was good.

great

skvělý

Great job!

hand

ruka

Please hand in your work.

help

pomoc

You should help others.

here

tady

Do you sit here?

home

domov

Is this your home?

house

dům

The doll house was pink.

just

prostě

The train just left.

kind

být milý

Be kind to each other.

know

znát

I don't know.

land

farma

They bought some land.

large

velký

A bear is large.

learn

učit se

It's fun to learn science.

letter

dopis

He mailed a letter.

line

linky

Please form a line.

little

málo

He has a little sister.

live

žít

You live in the city.

man

muž

The man drove.

me

mě

Come with me to the park.

means

prostředek

She got her by means of a taxi.

men

muži

The men played football.

most

většina

Most students like to help.

mother

matka

He loves his mother.

move

přestěhovat se

His family decided to move.

much

hodně

How much is the camera?

must

musí

You must raise your hand.

name	need
název	chtít
What is his name?	Do you need to sleep?
new	off
nový	vypnuto
We have a new teacher.	The rocket blasted off.
old	only
starý	pouze
Those are old toys.	There's only one slice left.

our

náš

She was our teacher.

over

přes

He jumped over it.

page

stránka

Please turn the page.

picture

obrázek

They took their picture.

place

místo

This is my favorite place.

play

hrát si

Let's play together!

point

směřovat

Point the way.

put

dát

Please put the supplies away.

read

číst

Do you like to read?

right

že jo

That's a right triangle.

same

stejný

Did you get the same answer?

say

říci

What did you say?

sentence

věta

Complete the sentence.

set

soubor

Please set the table.

should

by měl

We should exercise.

show

ukázat

Show your work.

small

malý

The ladybug is small.

sound

zvuk

A bee makes a buzzing sound.

spell

hláskovat

Please spell the word.

still

ještě pořád

I still want ice skates.

study

studie

It's time to study.

such

takový

He is such a good dog.

take

vzít

Please take your seat.

tell

sdělit

She wanted to tell a secret.

things

věci

She washed a lot of things.

think

myslet si

Think about it.

three

tři

It's the number three.

through

přes

He was through with the race.

too

také

Do you like chocolate too?

try

snaž se

Try again, please.

turn

otočit se

Turn in your homework.

us

nás

She taught us.

very

velmi

He is a very good singer.

want

chtít

I want to ride my bike.

well

studna

You did well.

went

šel

We went to recess.

where

kde

Where do you want to go?

why

proč

She asked why?

work

práce

Hard work pays off.

world

svět

I want to travel the world.

years

let

You are five years old today.

above

výše

The sky was above them.

add

přidat

If you add one plus two, you get three.

almost

téměř

It's almost lunch time.

along

podél

We get along.

always

vždy

She always brushes her teeth.

began

začal

The baby began to cry.

begin

začít

You may begin your exam.

being

bytost

She is being shy.

below

níže

It's below thirty degrees.

between
mezi

Two is between one and three.

book
rezervovat

I'm reading this book.

both
oba

They both worked on math.

car
auto

He bought a new car.

carry
nést

She had a bag to carry her groceries.

children
děti

Four children sang.

city
město

He worked in the city.

close
zavřít

Please close the door.

country

země

Do you live in the country?

cut

střih

You use scissors to cut.

don't

ne

Don't forget!

earth

země

Our planet is Earth.

eat

jíst

I eat bananas.

enough

dost

Did you eat enough pancakes?

every

každý

I shower every day.

example

příklad

This is an example of a bird.

eyes

oči

What color are her eyes?

face

tvář

They were at the face painting booth.

family

rodina

How big is your family?

far

daleko

How far is it?

father

otec

Her father walked her to school.

feet

chodidla

Put socks on your feet.

few

málo

She wanted a few more minutes.

food

jídlo

They made a lot of food.

four

čtyři

There were four of them.

girl

dívka

The girl wore pink shoes.

got

dostal

She got a hair cut.

group

skupina

They were working in a group.

grow

růst

The plant began to grow.

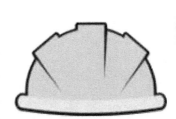

hard

tvrdý

He wore a hard hat.

head

hlava

He wore a cap on his head.

hear

slyšet

You hear through your ears.

high
vysoký

She wore high heels.

idea
idea

I have an idea!

important
důležité

It's important!

Indian
indický

It's an Indian elephant.

it's
je

It's a tiger cub.

keep
držet

Can you keep a secret?

last
poslední

It's the last day of school.

late
pozdě

You're late.

leave

odejít

He packed to leave.

left

vlevo, odjet

Are you left or right handed?

let

nechat

Will you let me go fishing?

life

život

Life is about friends and family.

light

světlo

The light turned yellow.

list

seznam

Here's my to-do list

might

mohl

It might rain today.

mile

míle

It's a mile from here.

miss

slečna, minout

You may correct any you miss.

mountains

hora

There are alot of mountains here.

near

u

We are near the beach.

never

nikdy

I've never broken my leg.

next

další

Take the next step.

night

noc

You can see the stars at night.

often

často

How often do you watch tv?

once

jednou

Once upon a time...

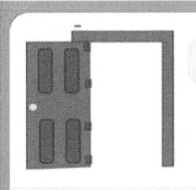

open

otevřeno

The door is open.

own

vlastní

Do you own a computer?

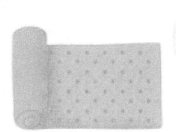

paper

papír

Do you have paper towels?

plant

rostlina

I will water the plant.

real

nemovitý

Her real name is Sally.

river

řeka

The river is high.

run

běh

He likes to run with his dog.

saw

vidět

We saw a UFO.

school

škola

Do you like school?

sea

moře

The ship is at sea.

second

druhý

She won second place.

seem

zdát se

You seem busy.

side

boční

Each side of a square is the same.

something

něco

Did you hear something?

sometimes

někdy

Sometimes we watch tv.

song

píseň

We will sing a song.

soon

již brzy

Dinner will be ready soon.

start

start

Start writing.

state

stát

Which state do you live in?

stop

stop

Do you see the stop sign?

story

příběh

What's the story about?

talk

mluvit

Let's talk.

those

ty

Those are great cookies!

thought

myslel

I thought the novel was good.

together

spolu

They went shopping together.

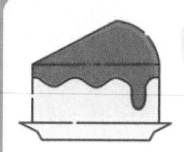

took

vzít

He took the last piece.

tree

strom

Did you decorate the tree?

under

pod

It lives under the sea.

until

dokud

I work until 5 o'clock.

walk

procházka

We went for a walk.

watch

náramkové hodinky

Do you wear a watch?

while

zatímco

We had fun while skiing.

white

bílý

They drew on the white board.

without

bez

I can't go without my backpack.

young

mladá

Her kids are young.

across

přes

It's across the street.

against

proti

It's against the rules.

area

plocha

There are no wild animals in this area.

become

stát se

It will become a butterfly.

best

nejlepší

Do your best!

better

lepší

Feel better soon!

birds

pták

There's a lot of birds.

black

černá

He has a black cat.

body

tělo

The body has a lot of bones.

certain

určitý

Certain words are harder than others.

cold

studený

It's cold outside.

color

barva

What is your favorite color?

complete

kompletní

Did you complete your workout?

covered

pokrýt

Snow covered the car.

cried

plakat

She cried.

didn't

ne

I didn't know.

dog

pes

My dog is cute.

door

dveře

The door was open.

draw

kreslit

Do you like to draw?

during

během

We learn a lot during class.

early

rychle

She had to get up early.

easy

snadný

He thought it was easy.

ever

vůbec

Don't ever doubt yourself!

fall

podzim

Be careful to not fall.

farm

přistát

They have cows on the farm.

fast

rychle

A cheetah is fast.

field

pole

It's the new football field.

figure

postava

Who was able to figure it out?

fire

oheň

We made a fire.

fish

ryba

Do you like fish?

five

pět

There are five of them.

friends

přátelé

They are my friends.

ground

přízemní

Grass covered the ground.

happened

stalo

What happend?

heard

slyšel

I heard you like music.

himself

sám

He smiled to himself.

hold

držet

Hold on to the balloons!

horse

kůň

Have you ever ridden a horse?

hours

hodin

How many hours is it open?

however

ale

He hates milk, however he drank it.

hundred

sto

She made a one hundred on the quiz.

I'll

vůle

I'll call.

king

král

Have you ever met a king?

knew

věděl

She knew the doctor.

listen

poslouchat

Do you listen to music?

low
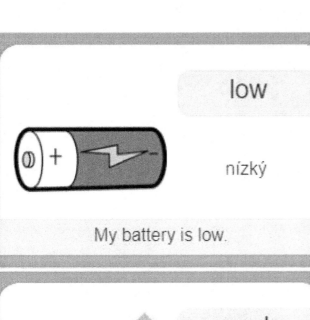
nízký

My battery is low.

map

mapy

Did you look at the map?

mark
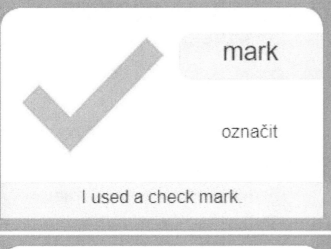
označit

I used a check mark.

measure
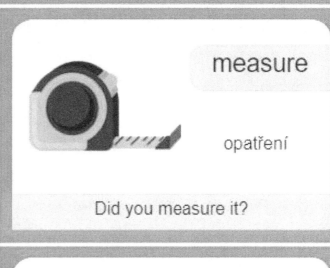
opatření

Did you measure it?

money

peníze

How much money have you saved?

morning

ráno

Do you drink coffee in the morning?

music

hudba

I love music.

north
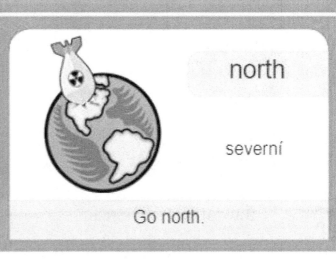
severní

Go north.

notice

oznámení

Put the notice on the board.

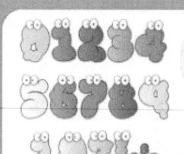

numeral

číslice

Which numeral did you choose?

order

sekvence

Put them in order of date.

passed

prošel

She passed her driver's exam.

pattern

vzor

Which dress pattern?

piece

kus

This piece fits.

plan

plán

Look at the house plan.

problem

problém

Let's solve the problem.

products

produkty

Which products do you like?

pulled

vytáhl

He pulled the wagon.

questions

otázky

Do you have questions?

reached

dosaženo

You reached high for your goals.

red

červené

It's a red heart.

remember

pamatovat

I'll try to remember.

rock

skála

A diamond is part of a rock.

room

pokoj, místnost

They hang out in this room.

seen

vidět

Have any of you seen the movie?

several

několik

They looked at several creatures.

ship

loď

The ship sailed.

short

krátký

You cut your hair short.

since

od té doby

Since you like cookies, let's make some.

sing

zpívat

We sing.

slowly

zpomalit

The turtle walked slowly.

south

jižní

Mexico is south of the US.

space

kosmos

The astronaut went to space.

stand

vydržet

Please stand up.

step

krok

Here's the step ladder.

sun

slunce

The sun was out.

sure

tak určitě

Sure, I'll go to the magic show!

table

stůl

Please sit at the table.

today

dnes

Today we'll go to the pool.

told

řekl

I told you I made a snowman.

top

horní

We put a cherry on top.

toward

k

She taught toward the front.

town

město

Meet at the town square.

travel

cestovat

Let's travel.

true

skutečný

It's true love.

unit

jednotka

A centimeter is a unit of length.

upon

na

Once upon a time there was a princess.

usually

obvyklý

Usually I have coffee.

voice

hlas

Use your quiet voice.

vowel

samohláska

What are vowels?

war

válka

The war of the Empire and the Republic.

waves

vlny

The waves were great for surfing.

whole

celý

Were you sick the whole time?

wind

vítr

The wind is too strong.

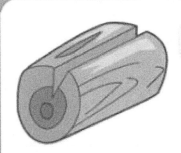

wood

dřevo

Did you chop the wood?

able

schopný

Are you able to ride a bike?

ago

před

It happened a long time ago.

am

to je

I am hungry.

among

mezi

He was among the chairs.

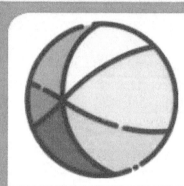

ball

míč

He was among the chairs.

base

baseball

Do you play first base?

became

stát se

She became a nurse.

behind

za

The cow was behind the fence.

boat

loď

Did you want to go on the boat?

box

krabice

What's in the box?

bring

přinést

Bring your friends!

brought

přinesl

Everyone brought a present.

building

budova

I made a building with legos.

built

postavený

He built a house.

cannot

nemůže

You cannot succeed without hard work.

carefully

opatrný

Handle those carefully.

check

šek

Did you get a check mark?

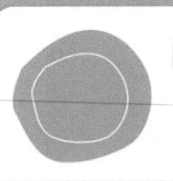

circle

kruh

She drew a circle.

class

třída

It's a class party.

clear

průhledná

The glass is clear.

common

všeobecné

They have a lot in common.

contain

obsahovat

What stories does it contain?

correct

opravit

Was that the correct piece?

course

chod

Did you go to the golf course?

dark

temný

It's dark at night.

decided

rozhodni se

We decided to go to the lake.

deep

hluboký

The ocean is very deep.

done

hotovo

Well done!

dry

suchý

Try to stay dry.

English

angličtina

Do you enjoy English class?

equation

rovnice

Find the answer to the equation.

explain

vysvětlit

Please explain it again.

fact

skutečnost

Is that a fact or opinion?

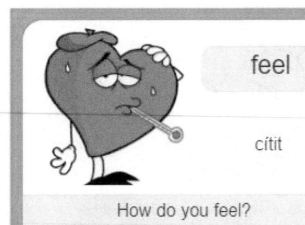

feel

cítit

How do you feel?

filled

plněné

It's filled with flowers.

finally

finále

She finally smiled.

fine

pokuta

He had to pay a fine.

fly

létat

Did you fly there?

force

platnost

We learned about force.

front

přední

She was at the front of the line.

full

plný

The basket was full.

game

hra

Who won the game?

gave

dal

He gave her flowers.

government

vláda

We learned about the government.

green

zelený

The frog is green.

half

polovina

I hate half the orange.

heat

teplo

Please heat up the oven.

heavy

těžký

It's really heavy.

hot

horký

The coffee is hot.

inches

palců

How many inches is it?

include

zahrnout

They made sure to include sunscreen.

inside

uvnitř

He was inside the dog house.

island

ostrovy

The island was beautiful.

known

znát

They've known each other forever.

language

jazyk

Do you know sign language?

less

méně

Three is less than five.

machine

stroj

It's grandma's sewing machine.

material

materiál

She needed material.

minutes

minut

How many minutes left?

note

poznámka

She left a note.

nothing

nic

He had nothing he had to do.

noun

podstatné jméno

Is that a noun or a verb?

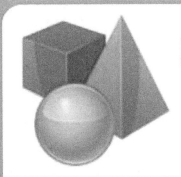

object

objekt

We measured each object.

ocean

oceán

I love the ocean.

oh

ach

Oh! It's a puppy!

pair

pár

Are those your pair of shoes?

person

osoba

He's a smart person.

plane

letadlo

Is it your first time on a plane?

power

napájení

What super power do you have?

produce

vyrobit

It will produce vegetables.

quickly

rychlý

The greyhound ran quickly.

ran

běžel

They ran the race.

rest

relaxovat

You needed to rest.

road

silnice

Is this the right road?

round

kolo

The soccer ball is round.

rule

pravidlo

Which rule did you break?

scientists

vědec

They are scientists.

shape

tvar

What shape is that?

shown

zobrazeno

The photo was shown to me.

six

šest

He rolled a six.

size

velikost

What's your shoe size?

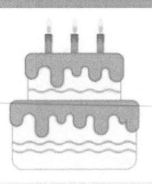

special

speciální

It's a special cake.

stars

hvězdy

How many stars did you earn?

stay

pobyt

She knows stay.

stood

stál

He stood at the teacher's desk.

street

ulice

It's on this street.

strong

silný

How strong are you?

surface

povrch

Most of the Earth's surface is water.

system

systém

Tell me about the solar system.

ten

deset

Did you hit all ten pins?

though

ačkoli

Even though she's busy, she read alot.

thousands

tisíce

Thousands of people live here.

understand

rozumět

Do you understand the homework?

verb

sloveso

Which word is a verb?

wait

počkejte

How long did you wait?

warm

teplý

How warm is the soup?

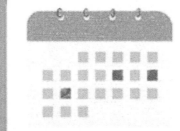

week

týden

This week is busy.

wheels

kola

Did you buy new wheels?

yes

ano

Yes, I want to go.

yet

dosud

Are we there yet?

anything

cokoliv

Do cows eat anything but grass?

arms

paže

She crossed her arms.

beautiful

krásná

The area is beautiful.

believe

věřit

I believe in Santa Claus.

beside

vedle

They stood beside one another.

bill

účtovat

Did you receive the bill?

blue

modrý

It's a blue butterfly.

brother

bratr

Is that your brother?

can't

nemůže

When I can't sleep, I count sheep.

cause

způsobit

What's the cause?

cells

buňky

We learned about cells.

center

centrum

The bullseye is the center.

clothes

oblečení

Did you hang your clothes up?

dance

tanec

They dance like professionals.

describe

popsat

Describe the colors.

developed

rozvíjet

They developed a strong friendship.

difference

rozdíl

What's the difference?

direction

směr

Which direction do we go?

discovered

objevit

Who discovered antibiotics?

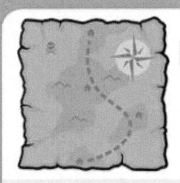

distance

vzdálenost

What's the distance to there?

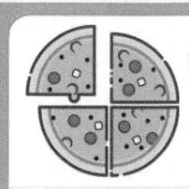

divided

rozdělit

It was divided up.

drive

řídit

Does your dad drive you?

drop

pokles

Did you drop and crack it?

edge

okraj

I stood at the edge of the pond.

eggs

vejce

Do you have enough eggs?

energy

energie

Have you used solar energy?

Europe

evropa

Are you going to visit Europe?

exercise

cvičení

We all should exercise.

farmers

farmáři

Farmers work hard.

felt

cítit

He felt happy with friends.

finished

dokončit

He finished his painting.

flowers

květiny

Flowers are growing there.

forest

les

Where is the forest?

general

všeobecné

We shopped at the general store.

gone

pryč

Has he gone fishing?

grass

tráva

Will you cut the grass?

happy

šťastný

Music made him happy.

heart

srdce

Did you draw a heart?

held

držet

They held hands.

instruments

nástroje

What instruments do you play?

interest

zájem

I have an interest in flowers.

job

práce

What job did you chose?

kept

držet

She kept hold of the balloon.

lay

položit

Will she lay an egg?

legs

nohy

A cricket has six legs.

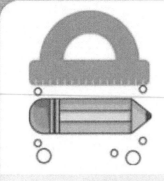

length

délka

What's the length?

love

milovat

Families love each other.

main

hlavní

There's the main gate.

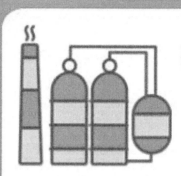

matter

hmota

What are the states of matter?

meet

setkat

Do you want to meet them?

members

členy

All the members were there.

million

milión

She watched a million how-to videos.

mind

mysl

Your mind is full of imagination.

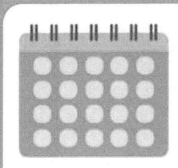

months

měsíce

There are several cold months.

moon

měsíc

The wolf howled at the moon.

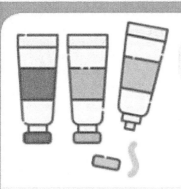

paint

malovat

What did you paint?

paragraph

odstavec

Have you written a paragraph?

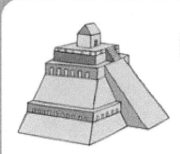

past

minulost

Archeology looks at the past.

perhaps

možná

Perhaps you want to go in it?

picked

vybral

They picked the book together.

present

současnost, dárek

Who is the present for?

probably

pravděpodobně

It's probably on the list.

race

závod

The race is about to begin.

rain

déšť

It started to rain.

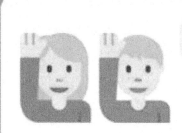

raised

zvedl

Everybody raised their hands.

ready

připraven

Is it ready?

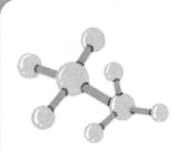

reason

důvod

Science uses logic and reason.

record

záznam

Who broke the record?

religion

náboženství

What religion is it?

represent

zastupovat

He drew pictures to represent words.

return

vrátit se

They were excited to return.

root

vykořenit

Which team do you root for?

sat

sedět

They sat and listened.

shall

musí

I shall ride this.

sign

podepsat

There's a stop sign.

simple

jednoduchý

It was a simple dress.

site

web

Have you looked at the site?

sky

nebe

The sky is clear.

soft

měkký

The teddy bear is so soft.

square

náměstí

A square has four equal sides.

store

ukládat

What store did you go to?

subject

předmět

What is your favorite subject?

suddenly

náhle

It happened suddenly.

sum

celkový

What is the sum of this?

summer

léto

Are you ready for summer?

syllables

slabiky

We are working on syllables.

teacher

učitel

The teacher read to them.

test

test

How'd you do on the test?

third

třetí

How did you like third grade?

train

vlak

We have a Christmas train.

wall

zeď

She painted the wall.

weather

#NAME?
západ

What is the weather like?

west

zda

You need to go west.

whether

široký

Whether you go by bus or not, go.

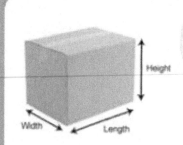

wide

divoký

How wide is the box?

wild

okna

What is your favorite wild animal?

window

zimní

Plants are in the window.

winter

přát si

Winter is here!

wish

psaný

Make a wish!

written

akt

It was written down.

act

afrika

Do you like to act in a play?

Africa

stáří

Did you vist Southern Africa?

age

již

They were around the same age

already

ačkoli

I already bought groceries.

although

množství

Although sunny, it's cold out.

amount

úhel

What amount of work do you have left?

angle

objevit

Please measure the angle.

appear

dítě

You appear to be lost.

baby

medvěd

Is this your baby?

bear

porazit

He loves his old teddy bear.

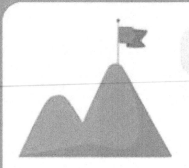

beat

lůžko

Our team beat yours.

bed

dno

We have a bunk bed.

bottom

jasný

There's treasure at the bottom.

bright

zlomený

The sun is really bright.

broken

stavět

Her heart is broken.

build

koupit

What are you going to build?

buy

péče

Did you buy a new car?

care

případ

She'll care for him.

case

kočka

Don't forget your case.

cat

století

I adopted a cat.

century

souhláska

They said it's a century old.

consonant

kopírovat

What is the consonant?

copy

nemůže

Is the copy machine working?

couldn't

počet

Couldn't we throw a fundraiser?

count

přejít

How high can you count?

cross

slovník

There's a cross on the church.

dictionary

zemřel

You may use a dictionary.

died

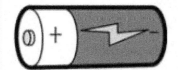

šaty

I didn't charge my phone and it died.

dress

buď

She loved her new dress.

either

každý

Will either of you wash the car?

everyone

všechno

Everyone was working.

everything

přesně

Everything here is fun.

exactly

faktory

It was exactly as she imagined.

factors

let

What are the factors of these numbers?

flight

prsty

The helicopter took flight.

fingers

podlaha

Cross your fingers.

floor

zlomek

Did you mop the floor?

fraction

volný, uvolnit

What fraction of the cake did you eat?

free

francouzština

They set the tiger free.

French

zlato

She's a French bull dog.

gold

vlasy

She had a gold star.

hair

kopec

Did you get get your hair cut?

hill

otvor

The sun peaked over the hill.

hole

naděje

Did you get a hole-in-one?

hope

led

Let's hope.

ice

namísto

The ice was melting.

instead

žehlička

Do you drink tea instead of coffee?

iron

skok

I need to iron my shirt.

jumped

zabil

The cow jumped over the moon.

killed

jezero

Pest control killed the bugs.

lake

zasmál se

We're still going to the lake.

laughed

vůdce

They all laughed.

lead

pojďme

We were in the lead.

let's

hodně

Let's go to the fair!

lot

melodie

The car lot was full.

melody

kov

What a beautiful melody.

metal

metoda

They have a metal trashcan.

method

střední

We use the scientific method.

middle

mléko

She stood in the middle.

milk

okamžik

Did you drink your milk?

moment

národ

Wait a moment for the bus.

nation

přírodní

Which nation are you from?

natural

mimo

This place has natural beauty.

outside

za

They brought sand in from outside.

per

fráze

It's forty dollars per car.

phrase

chudý

His phrase inlcuded a penny.

poor

možný

Did you do poor on the exam?

possible

liber

Will it be possible to grill this weekend?

pounds

tlačil

The price was in pounds.

pushed

klid

She pushed the stroller.

quiet

docela

Quiet in the library.

quite

zůstat

You are quite busy

remain

výsledek

Please remain in your seat.

result

jízda

What was the result of the election?

ride

válcované

Let's ride bikes!

rolled

plachta

The diploma was rolled up.

sail

stupnice

Do you like to sail?

scale

sekce

Use the scale to weigh them.

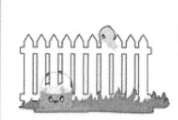

section

spát

This section is fenced off

sleep

usmál se

It's time to sleep.

smiled

sníh

He always smiled

snow

půda

Let's play in the snow!

soil

řešit

Plant it in the soil.

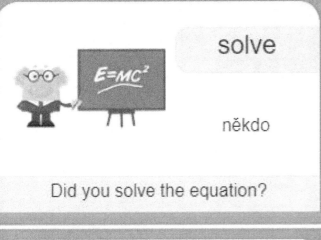

solve

někdo

Did you solve the equation?

someone

syn

Someone cleaned their desk.

son

mluvit

Is that your son?

speak

rychlost

Who will speak next?

speed

jaro

What's the speed limit?

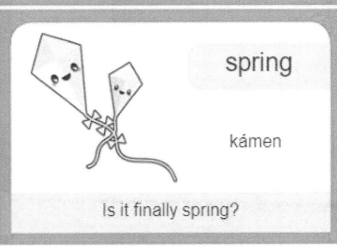

spring

kámen

Is it finally spring?

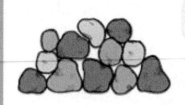

stone

překvapení

She skipped a stone across the pond.

surprise

vysoký

She threw a surprise party.

tall

teplota

How tall is a giraffe?

temperature

oni sami

What's the temperature?

themselves

malý

They enjoyed themselves.

tiny

výlet

It's so tiny.

trip

typ

Did you enjoy your road trip?

type

vesnice

What type of project is it?

village

v rámci

We travled to the village.

within

divit se

What did you see within the museum.

wonder

sama

I wonder what we'll see!

alone

umění

While alone, he read.

art

špatný

Do you like to look at art?

bad

banka

The movie was bad.

bank

bit

I need to go to the bank.

bit

přestávka

I bit the apple.

break

hnědý

Time for a break.

brown

hořící

It's a brown cow.

burning

podnikání

The candles were burning.

business

kapitán

They opened their business.

captain

úlovek

Who is the ship's captain?

catch

chycen

Did you catch the ball?

caught

centů

You caught a fish.

cents

dítě

That's just my two cents.

child

vybrat

The child prayed.

choose

čistý

Which one did you choose?

clean

vylezl

Did you clean?

climbed

mrak

They climbed it.

cloud

pobřeží

We watched the storm cloud.

coast

pokračoval

The coast is relaxing.

continued

řízení

He continued to look through the box.

control

chladný

Who has the remote control?

cool

náklady

That's a cool car.

cost

desetinný

They cut the cost.

decimal

poušť

Where does the decimal go?

desert

design

Have you been to the desert?

design

přímo

Did you design this?

direct

výkres

Did you direct the film?

drawing

uši

Is that your drawing?

ears

východní

Did you get your ears pierced?

east

jiný

Are you from the east coast?

else

motor

Did you draw that or did someone else?

engine

anglie

The fire engine parked there.

England

rovnat se

I want to go to England.

equal

experiment

Does it equal four?

experiment

vyjádřit

What was your experiment?

express

pocit

They have express delivery.

feeling

klesl

He's feeling sick.

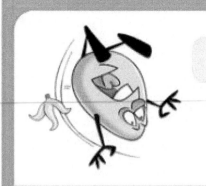

fell

tok

I fell down the stairs.

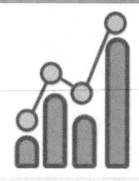

flow

chodidlo

We created a flow chart.

foot

zahrada

Twelve inches is a foot.

garden

plyn

She worked in the garden

gas

sklenka

We stopped to get gas.

glass

bůh

Did you clean the glass?

God

rostla

Many believe in God and angels.

grew

dějiny

The flower grew.

history

člověk

She taught history.

human

lov

We learned about the human body.

hunting

zvýšit

We're hunting for Easting eggs.

increase

informace

Did the house value increase?

information

sám

He took in so much information.

itself

připojil se

The house won't clean itself.

joined

klíč

I joined them at the cafe.

key

dáma

Did you find your key?

lady

zákon

The lady worked long hours.

law

nejméně

It's the law.

least

ztracený

Did you at least remember your bag?

lost

možná

Have you lost something?

maybe

pusa

Maybe we'll go rafting.

mouth

strana

Do your braces make your mouth hurt?

party

platit

How was the party?

pay

doba

We need to pay

period

pláně

You put a period at the end.

plains

prosím

The road went through the plains

please

praxe

Please have breakfast.

practice

prezident

They were at practice.

president

přijato

Make sure you vote for president

received

zpráva

She received an award.

report

prsten

Your report card looks great!

ring

stoupat

Such a beautiful ring!

rise

řádek

We were waiting for the sun to rise.

row

uložit

Did you go out on row boats?

save

semena

Try to save some money.

seeds

poslal

Did you get seeds for the garden?

sent

samostatný

Was the email sent?

separate

sloužit

The brain has separate parts.

serve

křičel

Did you serve that table?

shouted

singl

The cheerleaders shouted their cheer.

single

kůže

A single balloon

skin

prohlášení

She used a mask for her skin.

statement

lepit

He worked on his thesis statement.

stick

rovný

It's your hockey stick.

straight

podivný

It's a straight road.

strange

student

That's strange looking.

student

předpokládat

The students worked together

suppose

symboly

I suppose we could go to the pool.

symbols

tým

What do those symbols mean?

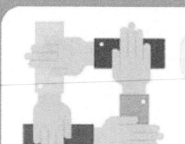

team

dotek

Are you on the basketball team?

touch

problémy

The cheerleader can touch her toes

trouble

strýc

Did you have car trouble?

uncle

údolí

We learned about Uncle Sam.

valley

návštěva

They traveled to the valley.

visit

mít na sobě

They went to visit their grandparents.

wear

jehož

Did you find a suit to wear?

whose

drát

Whose guitar is it?

wire

žena

This telephone has a wire.

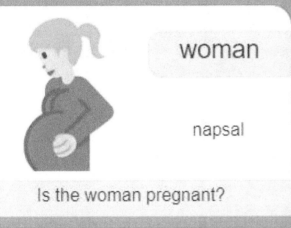

woman

napsal

Is the woman pregnant?

wrote

yard

She wrote poetry

yard

vy

Lucky is in the yard.

you're

vy sám

You're an angel.

yourself

přidání

Did you go hiking by yourself?

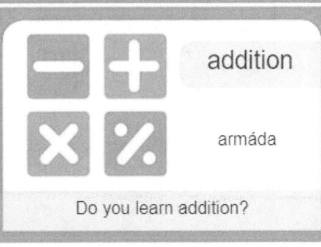

addition

armáda

Do you learn addition?

army

zvonek

Is he joining the army?

bell

patřit

Ring the bell.

belong

bloky

They belong together.

block

krev

Did you have a toy block?

blood

foukat

I donated blood.

blow

deska

Did you blow the bubbles?

board

kosti

That's her surf board

bones

větve

Did you see the dinosaur bones?

branches

dobytek

There are three branches.

cattle

hlavní

We raise cattle.

chief

porovnat

Is your dad the fire chief?

compare

sloučenina

You can't compare apples to oranges.

compound

zvážit

This is a compound.

consider

kuchařka

Did you consider it?

cook

roh

What did you cook?

corner

plodiny

Turn at that corner.

crops

dav

How are the crops growing?

crowd

proud

There was a large crowd.

current

doktor

Are these your current goals?

doctor

dolarů

He went to see the doctor.

dollars

osm

How many hundreds of dollars is it?

eight

elektrický

Did you hit the eight ball?

electric

elementy

Do you own an electric car?

elements

užívat si

Look at the periodic table of elements.

enjoy

vstoupil

Did you enjoy your coffee?

entered

až na

She entered the room.

except

vzrušující

like all vegetables except peas.

exciting

očekávat

This is so exciting!

expect

slavný

When do you expect the baby?

famous

vejít se

She's a famous actress.

fit

byt

How much did you fit in there?

flat

ovoce

The tire was flat.

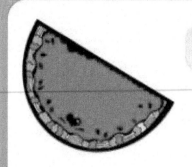

fruit

zábava

Watermelon is my favorite fruit.

fun

tipni si

They had fun at the beach

guess

čepice

Guess how many

hat

udeřil

I like your new hat.

hit

uveďte

They hit up a lot of stores.

indicate

průmysl

Did you indicate that you are ill?

industry

hmyz

This is where the industry is.

insects

zajímavý

Do you like insects?

interesting

japonský

The dog thought the toy was interesting.

Japanese

lhát

These are Japanese cherry blossoms.

lie

zvedl

It's never good to lie.

lifted

hlasitý

The jeep is lifted.

loud

hlavní, důležitý

The concert is loud.

major

nákupní centrum

What's your college major?

mall

maso

Do you want to go to the mall?

meat

těžit

Do you eat meat?

mine

moderní

Be mine.

modern

hnutí

She loves modern art.

movement

nutné

Movement is important.

necessary

pozorovat

It is necessary to go to school.

observe

park

Do you want to observe the stars?

park

konkrétní

Let's go to the park.

particular

planety

I prefer a particular ketchup.

planets

báseň

We were learning about the planets.

poem

pól

Would you read your poem?

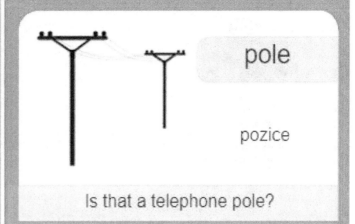

pole

pozice

Is that a telephone pole?

position

procesy

She likes sitting in that position.

process

vlastnictví

Is that the process?

property

poskytnout

That property is for sale.

provide

spíše

We wanted to provide food.

rather

rytmus

I'd rather be reading.

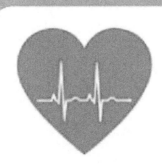

rhythm

bohatý

That's your heart's rhythm.

rich

bezpečný

I want to be rich.

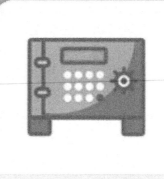

safe

písek

Do you have a safe?

sand

věda

They played in the sand.

science

prodat

We love science.

sell

poslat

She is going to sell lemonade.

send

smysl

Did you send the letter?

sense

sedm

What sense did you just use?

seven

ostrý

She has seven lipsticks.

sharp

rameno

Those are sharp scissors.

shoulder

povzdech

Did you hurt your shoulder?

sigh

tichý

Did you sigh?

silent

vojáci

Please be silent in the library.

soldiers

bod

They are soldiers.

spot

šíření

It's a red spot.

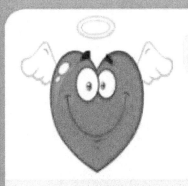

spread

proud

Spread your wings.

stream

tětiva

We played at the stream.

string

navrhl

It's a red string.

suggested

zásobování

I suggested you do your homework.

supply

plavat

Did you supply what you needed?

swim

podmínky

Let's go for a swim!

terms

tlustý

Did you learn new vocabulary terms?

thick

tenký

That's a thick book.

thin

tím pádem

That's a thin book.

thus

svázané

I was tired, thus I didn't go to the party.

tied

tón

Did you tie a knot?

tone

obchody

He said he's tone deaf.

trade

trubka

I'll trade you my sandwich for yours.

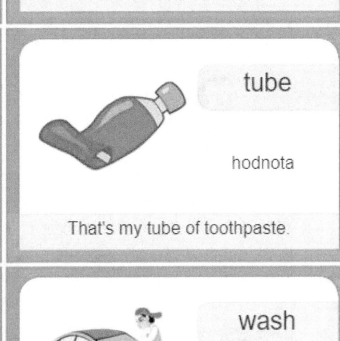

tube

hodnota

That's my tube of toothpaste.

value

praní

The value of family is greater.

wash

nebyl

We decided to wash the car.

wasn't

hmotnost

Wasn't that your cousin?

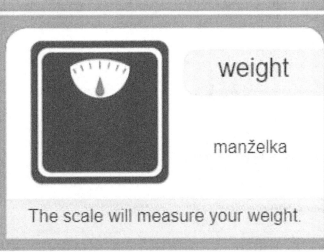

weight

manželka

The scale will measure your weight.

wife	wings
křídla	zvyklý
His wife is a teacher.	She was flapping her wings.

won't	a
jeden	o
Won't you go fishing with me?	A girl sang.

about	all
všechno	jeden
It's about lunch time.	It's all gone!

an	and
a	jsou
I have an idea!	I like cats and dogs.

are

tak jako

We are friends.

as

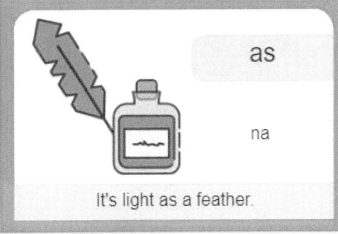

na

It's light as a feather.

at

být

You're at school.

be

byl

We'll be reading.

been

ale

I've been to Mexico.

but

podle

I like peas, but not cabbage.

by

volala

John sat by Jane.

called

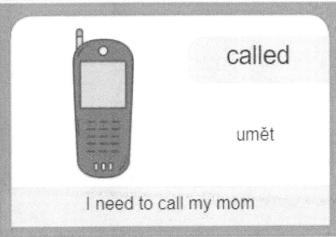

umět

I need to call my mom

can

přijít

Can you go to the zoo?

come

mohl

Will you come to the park?

could

den

Could you see the moon?

day

dělal

What day is it today?

did

dělat

Did you buy popcorn?

do

dolů

Do you like pizza?

down

každý

We walked down the stairs.

each

nalézt

They were one dollar each.

find

za prvé

Did you find your keys?

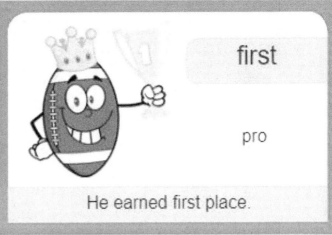

first

pro

He earned first place.

for

z

We ate turkey for Thanksgiving.

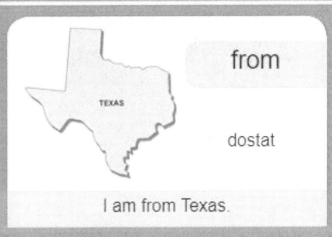

from

dostat

I am from Texas.

get

jít

Did you get your report card?

go

měl

May we go to recess?

had

má

Mrs. Smith had a cold.

has

mít

Lily has a cat.

have on Do you have a pencil?	**he** její he waved hello.
her mu It is her doll.	**him** jeho John sat next to him.
his jak It's his soccer ball.	**how** já How was the football game?
I #NAME? v I like icecream.	**if** do If you are sick, go see the nurse.

in

je

Halloween is in October.

into

to

That goes into the bin.

is

jako

It is hot outside

it

dlouho

It is raining.

like

dívej se

Do you like to read?

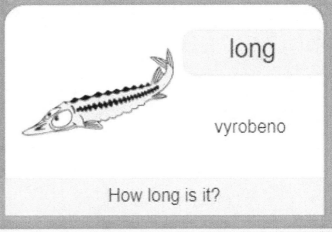

long

vyrobeno

How long is it?

look

udělat

Let's look at the stars.

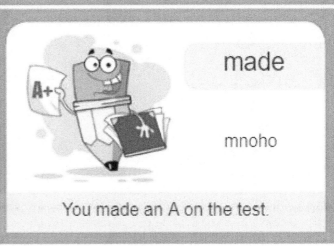

made

mnoho

You made an A on the test.

make

smět

We will make dinner.

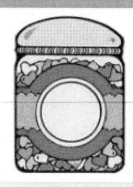

many

více

How many are in the jar?

may

můj

You may use the computer.

more

ne

I need more time.

my

ne

My favorite color is blue.

no

nyní

No talking in the library.

not

číslo

A giraffe is not short.

now

z

It's bedtime now.

number

olej

Her jersey number is twelve.

of

na

I'm proud of you!

oil

jeden

I changed the oil in my car.

on

nebo

Please turn on the light.

one

jiný

There is one cupcake left.

or

ven

Do you like cats or dogs?

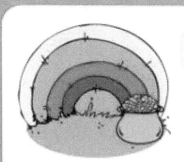

other

část

What other colors do we need?

out

lidé

Take the dog out for a walk.

part

řekl

He ate part of my homework.

people

vidět

Alot of people were dancing.

said

ona

She said hello.

see

sedět

He can't see without glasses.

she

tak

She had fun with her friends.

sit

nějaký

She decided to sit.

so

než

We had so much fun.

some

že

I need some paper.

than

jeden

He is taller than her.

that

jejich

That is my house.

the

jim

The weather is nice.

their

pak

They liked their teacher.

them

tam

I invited them to my party.

then

tyto

Do your chores, then you can play.

there

ony

It's over there.

these

tento

These are my markers.

they

čas

They were jump roping.

this

na

This is your backpack.

time

dva

What time is it?

to

nahoru

I went to school.

two

použití

There are two owls.

up

byl

We walked up the stairs.

use

voda

Let's use the pool.

was

cesta

She was reading.

water

my

Drink more water.

way

byly

It's a one way street.

we

co

We went to the beach.

were

když

We were at the carnival.

what

který

What is your question?

when

kdo

When is the dance?

which

vůle

Which snack do you want?

who

s

Who likes hockey?

will

slova

I will go to the park.

with

vůle

He had toast with his cereal.

words

napsat

You make words to play.

would

vy

Would you like some juice?

write

vaše

Please write your name.

you

You are strong.

your

Your ball is here.

Made in the USA
Las Vegas, NV
23 November 2020